Perfect your sigh

A workbook for exam

Piano Grade 1

Paul Harris

NAME		
EXAMINATION RECORD		
Grade	**Date**	**Mark**

TEACHER'S NAME
TELEPHONE

© 2000 by Faber Music Ltd
First published in 2000 by Faber Music Ltd
3 Queen Square London WC1N 3AU
Music and text set by Silverfen Ltd
Cover illustration by Drew Hillier
Printed in England by Caligraving Ltd
All rights reserved

ISBN 0-571-52021-9

To buy Faber Music publications or to find out about the full range of titles available
please contact your local music retailer or Faber Music sales enquiries:

Faber Music Limited, Burnt Mill, Elizabeth Way
Harlow, CM20 2HX. England
Tel: +44 (0)1279 82 89 82   Fax: +44 (0)1279 82 89 83
Email: sales@fabermusic.com   www.fabermusic.com

4.95

INTRODUCTION

It is arguable that the ability to sight-read is perhaps the most essential aspect of musicianship for the majority of both developing and established musicians. It is not too far-fetched to suggest that young players able to read music with the same degree of fluency and accuracy as words, would present their teachers with a rather different kind of challenge. Instead of continually correcting mistakes, more time could be spent on things *musical!*

Sight-reading is dependent on co-ordinating a number of processes all at the same time; this is a technique that can be both taught and developed. The human brain is quite capable of dealing with many thoughts and actions simultaneously; it's not at all uncommon in the helter-skelter lives we lead in today's busy world, and we can all do it! It is the ability to concentrate – to focus your mind on a task – that we must develop if sight-reading is to become really fluent and secure.

Using the workbook

You can use this workbook as a follow-on to **Improve your sight-reading! – Piano Grade 1.**

After two introductory stages, each stage is set out virtually identically to those in *Improve your sight-reading! – Piano Grade 1*. The **rhythmic exercises** help to develop the ability to feel and maintain a steady beat: clap or tap the lower line (the beat) while singing the upper line to 'la'; tap the lower line with your foot and clap the upper line, or tap the lower line with one hand and the upper line with the other.

The **melodic exercises** have been carefully devised to help you recognise melodic shapes – such as scales and arpeggios – at first glance. These begin with special exercises, written in semibreves, to help with note recognition; play these as slowly as necessary, and in your own time, in order to identify and correctly locate each note.

The **prepared pieces with questions** are to help you think about and understand the pieces before you play them. Put your answers in the spaces provided.

Finally, your teacher will give you an **unprepared text** to read at sight. Make sure you have read the *Sight-reading Checklist* on page 25 before you begin each piece.

Your teacher will mark your work according to accuracy. With the exception of the introductory stages, each stage carries a maximum of 50 marks and your work will be assessed as follows:

   2 marks for each of the six questions relating to the prepared piece (total 12).
   18 marks for the prepared piece itself.
   20 marks for the unprepared test. (Teachers can devise similar questions for the unprepared test, and take the answers into account when allocating a final mark.)

Space is given at the end of each stage for you to keep a running total of your marks as you progress. If you are scoring 40 or more each time you are doing well!

Don't forget to 'practise' the sight-reading pieces at home. Until a piece is really learned, there is still a strong element of sight-reading involved – even when the piece has been repeated a few times.

The really important factor is always to remember to concentrate – *feeling the pulse* and *thinking in the key.*

Take your sight-reading seriously – it will pay you great dividends.

The author wishes to thank Graeme Humphrey for many helpful suggestions.

STAGE 1

Do you ever watch television, eat a meal, and have a conversation simultaneously? Just think about it – three complicated activities happening *all at the same time*. Can you think of other situations where you're thinking and doing various things at once? It's not actually that difficult and it happens quite often.

Can you tap your head and rub your tummy in circles simultaneously? Now swap hands. If you managed this easily (both ways) then you probably won't find sight-reading difficult!

Here's a list of things you have to think about when sight-reading:

- keeping a steady pulse
- reading notes correctly
- understanding rhythmic patterns and combining them with notes
- remembering the key signature (if there is one)
- looking ahead
- observing dynamic markings and other expression marks
- fingering

A lot to think about, but don't be put off! The following exercises will get your brain used to thinking about and doing more than one task at a time. Practise until you can play them fluently and easily.

Play the upper line with your right hand while tapping the left-hand rhythm on your knee. Concentrate very hard as you play each exercise.

Now the right hand taps the rhythm:

© 2000 by Faber Music Ltd This music is copyright. Photocopying is illegal.

Think about the rhythm, and make sure that you observe the dynamic markings too!

Now play and then sing these two notes – the 1st (tonic) and 5th (dominant) of C major:

In the next exercises, sing the upper line while tapping the lower line.

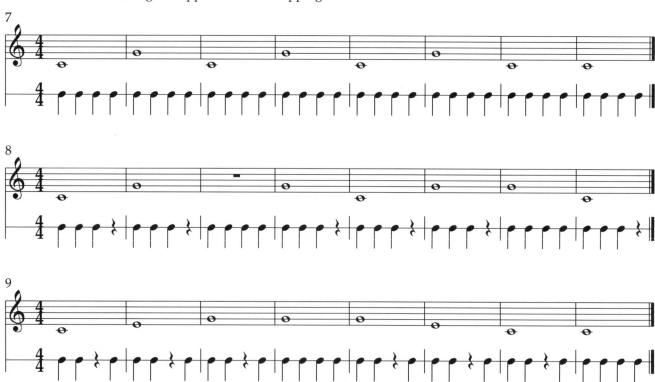

This time, sing the upper line and play the lower line. Remember to concentrate hard.

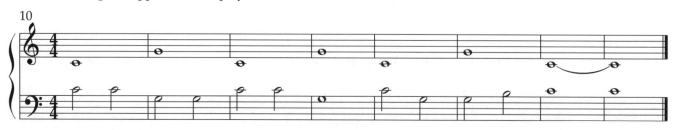

STAGE 2

Do you sometimes forget to look at the key signature when you're sight-reading? Playing in a key is a bit like speaking a foreign language – and it's best if you can try to think 'in the language'.

When you're playing a piece in say, B♭ major, you shouldn't be thinking C major plus a B♭ and an E♭, but really *thinking in B♭ major*. This ability will develop in time, but it will be considerably helped if you *force* yourself to think in the key, by concentrating on the key and its sharps and flats for a few moments before you begin playing.

But first of all it's very important that you KNOW your keys! Fill in the following table – it should take you about 30 seconds.

> The major key with no sharps or flats is _____ major
>
> The major key with 1 sharp is _____ major, and the sharp is _____
>
> The major key with 2 sharps is _____ major, and the sharps are _____ and _____
>
> The major key with 1 flat is _____ major, and the flat is _____
>
> The minor key with no sharps or flats is _____ minor
>
> The minor key with one flat is _____ minor, and the flat is _____

If you made any mistakes, copy out this table and try again.

Before you begin each of the following exercises you need to say the name of the key. Then SAY each of the notes rhythmically and out loud. Don't play this set of exercises.

Play the notes in each of the following exercises in your own time. Think of each note's name before you play it. As you play each exercise, remember to concentrate hard.

Before you begin, think: G major = F♯

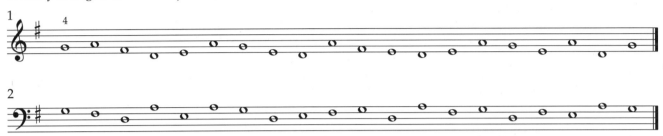

Before you begin, think: F major = B♭

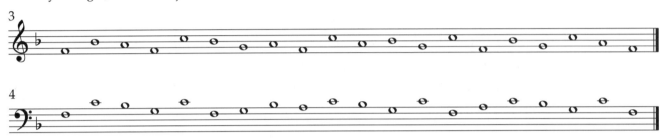

Before you begin, think: D major = F♯ and C♯

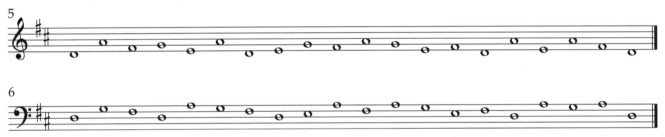

Before you begin, think: A minor = no key signature but some F♯ and G♯ accidentals

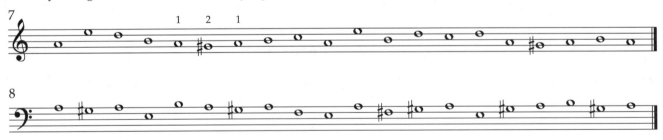

Before you begin, think: D minor = B♭ but some B♮ and C♯ accidentals

STAGE 3

C major

RHYTHMIC EXERCISES

1

2

3

MELODIC EXERCISES

Play the following notes in your own time (see Introduction).

1

2

Before you play each of the following, try to imagine what each piece sounds like in your head. Then sing the separate parts – first the right hand, then the left hand (at a comfortable pitch) – while tapping a crotchet pulse.

3 **Moderato**

4 **Like a waltz**

PREPARED PIECE

Marks*

1 What will you count? Clap through the whole piece.
   What is the rhythmic device joining the two G's (bars 1–2) called?

2 What key is this piece in?

3 What does *Allegretto* mean?

4 What do *f* (forte) and *p* (piano) indicate?

5 Try to hear the piece through in your head. Now sing the right-hand part out loud.

6 Clap the left-hand part through two or three times. Now try clapping it from memory.

Total:

Allegretto

Unprepared tests page 26

Mark:

Prepared work total:

Unprepared:

Total:

*The mark boxes are to be filled in by your teacher.

STAGE 4

G major

RHYTHMIC EXERCISES

MELODIC EXERCISES

Try to imagine what each piece sounds like in your head, then sing the right- and left-hand parts separately. Play the first note of each part before you begin singing.

Before you begin singing or playing, remember to *think in the key*!

PREPARED PIECE

1   What will you count? Clap through the whole piece.

2   What key is this piece in?

3   What does *Moderato* mean?

4   What do you notice about the A in bar 4?

5   Try to hear the piece through in your head. Now sing the right-hand part out loud.

6   Clap the left-hand part through two or three times. Now try clapping it from memory.

Total:

Moderato

Unprepared tests page 27

Mark:

Prepared work total:

Unprepared:

Total:

Running totals:

3	4

STAGE 5

F major

RHYTHMIC EXERCISES

MELODIC EXERCISES

Allegretto

Andante

PREPARED PIECE

1   What will you count? Clap through the whole piece.

2   What key is this piece in? How many B flats are there?

3   What does *Andante* mean?

4   What do you notice about bar 4 and bar 8?

5   Try to hear the piece through in your head. Now sing the right-hand part out loud.

6   Clap the left-hand part through two or three times. Now try clapping it from memory.

Total:

Andante

Unprepared tests page 28   Mark:

Prepared work total:

Unprepared:

Total:

Running totals:

3	4	5

STAGE 6

D major

RHYTHMIC EXERCISES

1

2

3

MELODIC EXERCISES

1

2

3 **Moderato**

4 **Con moto**

PREPARED PIECE

1   What will you count? Clap through the whole piece.

2   What key is this piece in? How many notes are affected by the key signature?

3   What does *Con moto* mean?

4   What rhythmic device is used in bars 1–2, 3–4 and 7–8?

5   Try to hear the piece through in your head. Now sing the left-hand part out loud.

6   Clap the right-hand part through two or three times. Now try clapping it from memory.

Total:

Con moto

Unprepared tests page 29

Mark:

Prepared work total:

Unprepared:

Total:

Running totals:

3	4	5	6

STAGE 7

A minor

RHYTHMIC EXERCISES

1

2

3

MELODIC EXERCISES

1

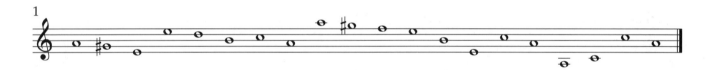

2

3

Moderato

PREPARED PIECE

1 What will you count? Clap through the whole piece.

2 What key is this piece in? Why are there F and G sharps?

3 How will the marking *Like a march* affect your performance?

4 In which other bars is the rhythm in bar 1 repeated?

5 Try to hear the piece through in your head. Now sing the right-hand part out loud.

6 Clap the left-hand part through two or three times. Now try clapping it from memory.

Total:

Like a march

Unprepared tests page 30

Mark:

Prepared work total:

Unprepared:

Total:

Running totals:

3	4	5	6	7

STAGE 8

D minor

RHYTHMIC EXERCISES

1

2

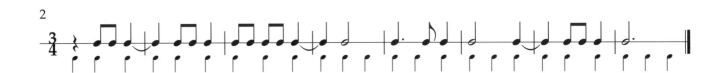

3

MELODIC EXERCISES

1

2

3 **Allegretto**

PREPARED PIECE

1 What will you count? Clap through the whole piece.

2 What key is this piece in? What is the name of the final note in bar 2?

3 How will the marking *Maestoso* affect your performance?

4 Where is the rhythm in bar 2 repeated?

5 Try to hear the piece through in your head. Now sing the left-hand part out loud.

6 Clap the right-hand part through two or three times. Now try clapping it from memory.

Total:

Unprepared tests page 31

Mark:

Prepared work total:

Unprepared:

Total:

Running totals:

3	4	5	6	7	8

A SIGHT-READING CHECKLIST

Piano Grade 1

Before you play a piece at sight always do the following:

1   Look at the time signature and decide how you will count the piece.

2   Look at the key signature, and begin to *think in the key*.

3   Decide which finger will start each phrase.

4   Notice any accidentals occurring during the piece.

5   Notice any scale and arpeggio patterns.

6   Work out leger-line notes if necessary.

7   Notice dynamic levels and other markings.

8   Decide what the character of the music is and how you will best achieve this.

9   Look at the tempo mark and any obvious technical difficulties and, taking both into account, decide what speed to play.

10 Count at least one bar in (in your head) before you begin, to establish the pulse.

When performing your sight-reading piece, remember to:

1   Continue to count and think in the key throughout the piece.

2   Keep going at a steady and even tempo.

3   Ignore mistakes.

4   Look ahead – at least to the next note or beat.

5   Play expressively and try to give character to your performance; in other words, play *musically*.

6   **CONCENTRATE!**

Handwritten annotations:

Xmas cake

cake

marzipan

icing

(1) Time signature
(2) Key signature
(3) Pitch letter names & height or depth on the 5 lines
(4) any patterns eg triads
(5) Speed can be slower if more accurate
(6) dynamics
(7) staccato legato

UNPREPARED TESTS
Before you begin, go through the *Sight-reading Checklist*, page 25

STAGE 3

STAGE 4

STAGE 5

STAGE 6

STAGE 7

homework   1   a   day

STAGE 8

Are you paralysed with fear
every time you go on stage?

Discover how to turn nerves
to your advantage.

CONFIDENCE-BOOSTING STRATEGIES
for musicians and performers

KEEPING
YOUR
NERVE!

Kate Jones

FABER *ff* MUSIC

3. If you are not a pianist, try and make sure you have as much practice with your accompanist as possible. It's important that you know the accompaniment as well. After all, it is part of the music! And don't be afraid of your accompanist. You are the soloist and they are there to make music with you. The same goes for ensemble playing. Getting to know your colleagues and how they may deal with nerves is as important as practising the notes.

Don't be afraid of your accompanist ...

4. If you are playing several pieces in your recital and you are able to devise the programme order, it is often helpful to start with a piece you know well or a piece that isn't too technically demanding. This way you allow yourself the best warming-up conditions and are more likely to control your nerves.

5. Make sure you like the music you are playing. Enjoying what you do is another key element to reducing any nerves you may feel. It's your performance and you need to be in control.

12

8. Allow ... predict what mig ... contingency plan so that if you ... sitting around. See if there is a park or a café nearby where you could use any spare time you have doing something not connected with the impending performance. Above all, use the time to relax.

Allow plenty of time to get to the venue, as you can never predict what might happen en route ...

13

Keeping your nerve! is the perfect prop for the young or amateur performer affected by stage fright. Full of comforting, easy-to-find advice and amusing anecdotes, this book will help you to:

· prepare for your performance, whether for a concert or exam
· enjoy performing, wherever and whenever
· unwind after the performance
· understand why you perform and why your audience turns up

Kate Jones also teams up with a star-studded cast of sympathetic performers and teachers, including Joanna MacGregor, Elvis Costello and Steven Isserlis, who reveal the special tactics that prevent them from turning to jelly!

"An invaluable, wonderful book. This must be in every musician's hands, young or old!"
(*Evelyn Glennie*)

Keeping your nerve!   ISBN 0-571-51922-9